If I'm So Good, Why Don't I Act That Way?

JUDITH COUCHMAN

NAVPRESS ®
A DIVISION OF THE NAVIGATORS
P.O. BOX 6000, COLORADO SPRINGS, COLORADO 80934

NavPress publishes materials with practical and
spiritual insights for everyday living.

ISBN 08910-93214

QUESTIONS WOMEN ASK series edited by Judith
Couchman.

This series helps women explore practical and
spiritual answers to urgent questions.

Printed in the United States of America

FOR A FREE CATALOG OF
NAVPRESS BOOKS & BIBLE STUDIES,
CALL TOLL FREE 1-800-366-7788 (USA)
or 1-416-499-4615 (CANADA)

CONTENTS

For Christie,
who lives with passion and creativity,
and who never allows
differences in faith
to mar our friendship.

ACKNOWLEDGMENTS

E ven a small book needs many people con-
nected to its development. So I'd like to
thank these faithful supporters:

Opal Couchman, Shirley Honeywell, and
Barbara Mortensen, family members who
always express interest in my work.

Charette Barta, Madalene Harris, Mae
Lammers, Nancy Lemons, Jeanine McArthur,
Gerry Woodward, and others who pray for my
writing projects.

Claudia Stafford and Debby Weaver, who
patiently assist in shaping my manuscripts.

Dan Rich, who insists on creating fresh
ways to help people find faith. ■

Are You Tired of Falling Short?

This book can renew your lost hope.

D *o you feel there's a chasm between who you are and who you'd like to be? If so, keep reading.*

As a young man, the famous photographer Ansel Adams played the piano quite well. Once, at a party he called "very liquid," Adams performed Chopin's F Major Nocturne.

"In some strange way my right hand started off in F-sharp major and my left hand behaved well in F major," he recalled. "I could not bring them together. I went through the entire nocturne with the hands separated by a half-step."

The next day a fellow guest told him, "You never missed a wrong note!"[1]

Do you sometimes feel you're never missing a wrong note? That your mistakes are pretty stupid? That no matter how hard you try, you always fall short?

You're not alone. All of us struggle with the person we are versus the person we'd like to be. We'd feel lucky if we could contain the struggle in the privacy of our souls, late at night. But

7

usually it bursts forth during daylight in the form of personal actions that confuse, embarrass, even horrify us. And often we have only ourselves to blame.

Missing Message

Falling short of personal expectations varies from person to person, and so do the results of our unwanted actions. But the ensuing shame, self-doubt, and frustration feel the same. In the end we're all left asking, "If I'm so good, why don't I act that way?"

It's as if, deep in our hearts, we know that somehow we were meant to be perfect. But somewhere along the way, things messed up and our minds and bodies didn't get the message.

There's a reason we feel this way—and a solution for this painful dilemma. But first we must open up to the God of the universe and his redemptive plan. You can learn about him—and his life-changing gift for you—in this study book.

First, an article explores the question, "Why is it so hard to be human?" Then four study lessons present the way to tackle inward sins that affect outward actions. After the lessons, appendix sections provide additional insights and help.

So if you question your perplexing actions, turn the page. The answer might be only a half-step away. ∎

— JUDITH COUCHMAN

NOTE
1. Clifton Fadiman, ed., *The Little, Brown Book of Anecdotes* (Boston, MA: Little, Brown and Company, 1985), page 5.

Why Is It So Hard to Be Human?

Why we don't act the way we want to.

O*ften when we least expect it, our character flaws can whack us in the face. Why is it that, even when we need to the most, we can't trust ourselves?*

"You're so selfish! You never listen to what I say! I've done all this work for you, and you don't even care!"

"Oh, yeah? Well, you're just too demanding! Everybody says you're awfully hard to work for!"

"Don't throw that 'everybody' stuff at me! *I dare you* to name names. . . ."

Two angry, accusatory voices ricocheted down the office halls. And one of them was mine.

I'd known this committee meeting might be difficult, but I hadn't expected the surprising turn it took, leaving me dismayed and defenseless. For the last hour of the agenda, I'd felt my anger building toward the chairperson, but managed to stave it off. Now, with everybody gone but us, we verbally ripped into each other like wildcats hungry for blood.

So much for my professionalism. It was the worst fight of my life: a yelling, fist-pounding confrontation. And I was too tired, too over-worked, to care about how this battle would damage me, my coworker, and our relationship.

That is, until I tossed in bed that night, tearfully blinking at the darkness. Then I accused myself: *Why in the world did I behave that way? I must be a horrible person to yell like that. Why can't I act the way I want to?*

Revealing Actions

It's been said that "adversities do not make the person either weak or strong, but they reveal what he is."[1] That's not a comforting thought when inward pressures turn into less-than-admirable actions. It's painful to lose control and not act the way we really want to. During those times, we'd rather do most anything than peer inside and greet our imperfect selves.

Interestingly enough, it's not just the knockout fights, the damaging faux pas, that can shame us. From talking too much to binge-ing on food to hurting our children, we're frustrated when we fail to do the "right" thing; when no matter how hard we try, our actions don't reflect our good intentions.

Unfortunately, age and maturity don't always close the gap between who we are and who we'd like to be.

"You know, I've read that *who you really are* intensifies as you grow older," a thirty-something friend worried aloud to me. "That means the sweet people will get sweeter. But I'm afraid I'm going to be an unbearable old lady, because I can be so demanding now!"

Of course, with self-discipline my friend can work on her outer actions. But she's hit on something that we all know: A polished exterior only camouflages an interior self that can be tricky to control.

It's not that we're all bad to the bone. Instead, we're dichotomies of love and hatred, kindness and selfishness, forgiveness and vengeance. But we like to believe we exhibit more of our good characteristics than the bad. Consequently, when darker traits move forward to create havoc, we startle even ourselves. Staring at the emotional and relational debris, we ask, "If I'm so good, why don't I act that way?"

Mythic Self-Stories

Often we can't—or don't want to—contemplate this question. The answer might be too revealing, too painful, to comfortably live with ourselves. So we create self-stories, based on half-truth and half-denial, to cope with who we are.

Rather than accepting that we're both good and bad, we often swing the self-descriptive pendulum from one end to the other. We might gravitate toward only what we do right, refusing to acknowledge or take responsibility for wrongful actions. Or we can wallow in self-loathing, always berating and never loving ourselves. Either way, we live in denial—and can repel people from us.

Take, for example, Sarah and Wendy.[2]

When Sarah got married, she expected

11

hearts and flowers forever. Then a few months after the wedding, Sarah's husband, Gary, gently pointed to some thorny things about her.

Instead of listening, Sarah shot back, "I don't do that, and you know it! Besides, you aren't always so hot yourself!"

"But honey, I only meant it to help," he started.

"Well, I don't need that kind of help," she snapped, walked into the bedroom, and slammed the door. Two years later, their marriage totters on the edge of divorce. As long as Gary ignores Sarah's weaknesses, everything's fine. But Gary's wearing thin over Sarah's refusal to face herself.

On the other hand, Wendy hoped marriage would erase her poor self-image. Instead, it enhanced Wendy's obsession with her personal weaknesses.

"I'm such an awful wife," she sobbed after overdrawing the checkbook.

"It's not the end of the world," said her husband Larry. "We'll survive."

Still crying, Wendy asked, "How can you stand me?" Larry offered comfort, but as Wendy's self-berating has continued through the years, he's stopped trying to console her. Now he retreats to the television or anywhere else to avoid the harangue.

Both Sarah and Wendy spin deceptive tales about themselves. Sarah believes she's all good; Wendy insists she's all bad. Whether they deny or admit it, neither woman acts the way she wants to. They're disappointed in the person who resides within.

Wilhelm Grimm, the compiler of ancient fairy tales, said the mythic element of stories resembles "small pieces of a shattered jewel which are lying strewn on the ground all overgrown with grass and flowers, and can only be discovered by the far-seeing eye."[3] This description also fits human nature, which in reality, is a tangled web of hidden gems and overgrown weeds. And the myths we create about ourselves can be difficult for us to see.

Viewing Ourselves

To close the gap between our intentions and actions, we must first realistically look at ourselves, flaws and all, and acknowledge that we don't like the whole view. The first look focuses on actions, feelings, attitudes — the expression of who we are and what's inside us.

Once, during an unsettling season of personal anger, I locked myself into a hotel room and wrote long lists of why I felt so mad. For a couple of hours, I scribbled everything from the rude to the ridiculous on an oversized legal pad. My list included items like this:

I'm unhappy with the way I look.

I'm mad at chauvinistic decisions in the workplace.

I'm frustrated because there's so much suffering in the world.

I'm still angry over losing my job a few years ago. It messed me up.

13

I'm angry because Sherry didn't give me a birthday present, and I gave her one.

Rereading the list later, the root of my anger glared back at me. I wanted to have control over my life: the events, the people, the outside circumstances. I resented their unexpectedly barging in and hurting me, their thwarting my goals and making me unhappy.

Because I couldn't control those aspects of life, I did the next powerful thing: I got angry. And while those around me chalked it up to a strong-willed woman, I knew it really spilled from a hurting inner child.

So we must take a second look at ourselves. With a "far-seeing eye," we need to examine our personal history and current circumstances for the hidden causes of our unwieldy actions. Although many internal reasons exist for these behaviors, we can begin by examining several common possibilities.

Family Behaviors

Not long ago, a neighbor mentioned she'd just attended her son's school program—and wasn't happy with the results. The teacher had misdirected and embarrassed her son in front of the parental audience.

"Did he cry?" I asked, thinking about what I'd have done as a child.

"No, he clammed up and just stood there, staring at the teacher," she sighed. Then after a pause she admitted, "He acted just like I do with my husband. It's really horrible to see my own stubbornness in my son."

Whether it's through genetic or learned responses, we emulate nuclear family behaviors and unwittingly carry them through life. Like the silent son in the Christmas pageant, we're susceptible to patterning after our parents and siblings. And it can seem like their negative responses seeped inside us more than anything else.

We can also continue to play a role we fulfilled in the family circle. For example, if we played the family "star" and got mounds of attention, we could expect the same adulation from husbands, friends, or associates. However, most people in our adult lives didn't grow up with us and aren't programed to respond as our family members did. When the people around us fail to respond according to our expectations, we can inflict misery on everyone, including ourselves.

If we're not aware and watchful, the patterns and roles of the past can lure us toward humiliating actions.

Subverted Self-Esteem

In her book *Designing a Life*, Mary Catherine Bateson described her years as dean of the faculty at Amherst College. During that time, Mary observed the subversion of female faculty members. She explained:

> *The subversion was accomplished by taking advantage of two kinds of vulnerability that women raised in our society tend to have. The first is the quality of self-sacrifice, a learned willingness to set their own interests*

aside and be used and even used up by the community. . . .

The second kind of vulnerability trained into women is a readiness to believe messages of disdain and derogation. Even women who arrived at Amherst full of confidence gradually became vulnerable to distorted visions of themselves, no longer secure that their sense of who they were matched the perceptions of others. And all of this is available as a bad model for the next generation.[4]

These two vulnerabilities permeate the hearts of most women today; so do the subversion tactics used against us. Low self-esteem messages can begin within the family circle. But even with a loving, supportive home life, women emerge into a world that can devalue their personal and professional worth.

As the daughter of anthropologist Margaret Mead, Mary lived with an example of a woman's valuable, unconventional contribution to society. Yet Mary openly admitted, "I have slighted my own value so often that it is hard to learn to take it seriously. Instead, I get things done by finding rationales for the task and then sacrificing myself for it."[5]

Out of similar feelings of self-degradation, we can react in ways that perplex or even embarrass us.

Unresolved Hurt

During my season of anger, I unreasonably took on more than a colleague. I unleashed on my boss, a man who physically and professionally stood formidably above most. Luckily for me, his broad shoulders extended beyond the physical sense, and he didn't punish me for a ridiculous outburst.

"What was that all about?" he asked me days later when I'd turned my boiler down.

Though I couldn't answer him then, the question stuck with me. Eventually, I realized that I'd displaced my anger; I wasn't really mad at him. In the last year, I'd suffered the loss of a job and security. With the intensity of searching for work and moving to another state, I didn't have time to heal the hurt and dissipate my anger. But repressed frustration eventually explodes, and it spewed on this boss instead of the man who'd unjustly fired me.

Unresolved pain usually expresses itself in exacerbating and exasperating actions.

Unremitting Stress

Even though we complain that life is harried — that everyone's overworked and over-scheduled — we often stand helpless before stress. And the effects of continual stress stamp physical and psychological marks on us.

For the physical effects, consider the skin. "It not only mirrors human adjustment to the physical circumstances of life, but it's also a window into the individual's inner condition. Many people who come to the doctor seeking explanations of rashes, eruptions, or hives actually are often suffering from nothing more than stress, tension, and psychological unhappiness."[6]

Similarly, ongoing stress can affect us psychologically.

After I lambasted my colleague for his committee meeting, I knew it was time to reevaluate my schedule. Although I'd found a new job, it'd been like the proverbial "jumping out of the frying pan into the fire" in regard to workload. In addition, I was completing my master's degree, accepting freelance writing assignments, and helping plan a major conference.

I'd scheduled my life this way for several years, and now it'd caught up with me. I'd burned out, and the ongoing stress made me tense and defensive. To change who I'd become, I needed to drastically alter my schedule—and my expectations for myself.

We often forget that unremitting stress can magnify our weaknesses and erupt them into hard-to-control actions.

Lack of Discipline

We also behave poorly if we're too lazy to discipline ourselves. We may resist controlling our destructive behaviors—or solving their resultant problems.

Before his conversion to Christianity in the first century, Saint Augustine lived raucously. From his mother Monica's example, Augustine knew what an exemplary life looked like, but he couldn't paint that picture for himself.

In his book *Confessions*, Augustine recounted the sins of his youth and how his prayers rang with insincerity. "Give me chastity and continence," he told God, "but not yet."[7]

Like Augustine, we often keep from assuming responsibility for ourselves because of procrastination.

In his best-selling book *The Road Less Traveled*, psychiatrist M. Scott Peck explained that "all of us from time to time seek to avoid — in ways that can be quite subtle — the pain of assuming responsibility for our own problems."[8] He wrote of four disciplines necessary to change ourselves:

- **Delayed gratification:** scheduling the pain and pleasure of life in a way that faces the pain before enjoying the pleasure.

- **Acceptance of responsibility:** admitting and assuming responsibility for our personal problems.

- **Dedication to truth:** examining ourselves honestly, before ourselves and others.

- **Balancing:** striking a flexible balance between conflicting needs, goals, responsibilities, etc., to create appropriate responses.[9]

So to change the actions that plague us, it's necessary to take a third, extended look at ourselves. A look that takes time and chooses to suffer the pain of change.

Spiritual Help

We may determine to change by ourselves or with the expert help of others, but these efforts are limited without looking at our spiritual selves. Each of us houses a soul (the mind, will, emotions) and a spirit that lives after our bodies die. God created us with a spiritual dimension so we could enjoy and communicate with him forever.

Yet early in time, a barrier erected against our relationship with God and the freedom to live unhindered by personal afflictions. It was sin: humanity's rebellion against God and his moral laws. When we unearth the causes for our problems, we find sin tangled in the roots.

The good news is that God wants to rescue us from sin—and from the inability to trust ourselves and our actions. He can infuse us with his power so we can change and live fully. But first, we must believe and receive God's redemptive plan for us. You can learn more about this plan—and your part in it—in the Bible lessons that follow.

Without God's power to change me, I'd never have survived that season of anger—or have found forgiveness with the people I offended. With the ancient psalm writer I agree: "I would have despaired unless I had believed that I would see the goodness of the Lord."[10] And with that focus, we can begin changing our disappointing actions. ■

NOTES
1. Faith Forsythe in *Tid-Bits*, quoted by Frank S. Mead, *The Encyclopedia of Religious Quotations* (Old Tappan, NJ: Fleming H. Revell Company, 1965), page 1.
2. To protect identities in this book, I changed all names, altered revealing circumstances, and sometimes created composites.
3. Padraic Colum, Introduction to *The Complete Grimm's Fairy*

Tales (New York: Pantheon Books, 1944), page xiv.

4. Mary Catherine Bateson, *Composing a Life* (New York: Atlantic Monthly Press, 1989), pages 53-54.

5. Bateson, page 40.

6. Jonathan Zizmor, M.D., and John Foreman, *Super Skin* (New York: Thomas Y. Crowell Company, 1976), page 33.

7. Clifton Fadiman, ed., *The Little, Brown Book of Anecdotes* (Boston: Little, Brown and Company, 1985), page 28.

8. M. Scott Peck, M.D., *The Road Less Traveled* (New York: Simon and Schuster, 1978), page 40.

9. Peck, pages 18-69.

10. See Psalm 27:13.

Where's Your Faith?

There's someone you can really trust.

When you say or do regrettable things, it's tough to trust yourself.

But there's good news. You can trust God to help you through those perplexing times. He can change you deeply, so you're no longer afraid of who you are and what you do.

The following lessons will introduce you to the God you can trust. They're based on stories or principles from the Bible and make the following assumptions. (Bible verses that explain these assumptions appear in italics.)

1. God exists. *The living God is among you* (Joshua 3:10). God's Son, Jesus, was his representative to people on earth. *A voice came from heaven: "You [Jesus] are my Son, whom I love; with you I am well pleased"* (Luke 3:22).

2. God cares about individuals. He wants to be part of our daily lives, especially when we're struggling with personal issues. *"Do not fear, for I am with you; do not be dismayed, for I*

am your God. I will strengthen you and help you"
(Isaiah 41:10).

3. The Bible holds God's words to humanity. *All Scripture is God-breathed and is useful for teaching, rebuking, correcting and training* (2 Timothy 3:16).

4. God will help change us for the better if we ask him into our lives. *For it is God who works in you to will and to act according to his good purpose* (Philippians 2:13).

To complete each lesson, you'll need this book, a pen or pencil, and about forty-five minutes. Occasionally, you'll also need a Bible and a dictionary.

Even if you're skeptical, even if you don't understand everything, try the lessons. They'll introduce you to a personal God who loves you, understands your frustrations, and wants to help you become a better woman. ■

Scene of the Crime

How humanity veered
off track years ago.

M *y Goal: To discover the origin of my struggle with sin and disappointing actions.*

The introduction to this book said struggling against ourselves is like knowing "that somehow we were meant to be perfect. But somewhere along the way, things messed up and our minds and bodies didn't get the message."

God did create us to be perfect—and things did mess up along the way. In this lesson, meet the people who veered off track years ago and instigated the personal battle you fight today.

Before you begin, check your viewpoint on the Bible truths presented in this lesson.

Your Viewpoint

1. a. What is your view of God's relationship to humanity?

b. How do you believe the world and its people were created?

c. How do you think evil or sin entered the world?

Very Good Creations

"In the beginning. . . ."

You've probably heard this introduction to the Bible. These words begin the description of creation, when God made the earth and everything in it. He created the seas and dry land, the sun and moon, the animals and vegetation. (You may want to read about creation in Genesis 1:1-25 of a Bible.)

Then on the last day of his creative masterpiece, God formed man and woman in his image. The Bible continues the story:

Then God said, "Let . . . them [humans] rule over the fish of the sea and the birds of the air, over the livestock, over all the earth, and over all the creatures that move along the ground."

So God created man in his own image, in the image of God he created him; male and female he created them.

God blessed them and said to them, "Be fruitful and increase in number; fill the earth and subdue it. Rule over the fish of the sea and the birds of the air and over every living creature that moves on the ground."

Then God said, "I give you every seed-bearing plant on the face of the whole earth and every tree that has fruit with seed in it. They will be yours for food. . . ."

God saw all that he had made, and it was very good. (Genesis 1:26-29,31)

2. God originally created people and nature flawlessly. Adam and Eve didn't struggle with imperfections in themselves or the earth.

   a. Imagine a perfect woman. If she was created in God's image, what do you think she would be like?

   b. Would you like to be this perfect woman? Why, or why not?

3. Quickly review the Bible passage above (Genesis 1:26-29,31), then answer the following questions.

a. What responsibilities did God give to this man and woman?

b. What provisions did he give to them?

c. What could these duties and provisions tell you about God?

4. God looked at what he created and called it "very good."

   a. Think of something you created that was "very good." How did you feel about yourself and your creation?

   b. How do you think God felt about his creation?

Eye-Opening Decision
When God created Adam and Eve, he didn't make them puppets, controlling their actions.

He gave them responsibilities and decision-making abilities. Bible teachers call this right to choose a *free will*.

Satan, a fallen angel turned enemy of God, knew Adam and Eve each possessed a free will. So disguised as a serpent, he tempted them to disobey God:

> *The man and his wife were both naked, and they felt no shame.*
>
> *Now the serpent was more crafty than any of the wild animals the LORD God had made. He said to the woman, "Did God really say, 'You must not eat from any tree in the garden'?"*
>
> *The woman said to the serpent, "We may eat fruit from the trees in the garden, but God did say, 'You must not eat fruit from the tree that is in the middle of the garden, and you must not touch it, or you will die.'"*
>
> *"You will not surely die," the serpent said to the woman. "For God knows that when you eat of it your eyes will be opened, and you will be like God, knowing good and evil."*
>
> *When the woman saw that the fruit of the tree was good for food and pleasing to the eye, and also desirable for gaining wisdom, she took some and ate it. She also gave some to her husband, who was with her, and he ate it.*
>
> *Then the eyes of both of them were opened, and they realized they were naked; so they sewed fig leaves together and made coverings for themselves.* (Genesis 2:25–3:7)

5. Why do you think the forbidden fruit appealed to Eve?

6. How did personal choice and pressure from others affect Eve's and Adam's disobedience?

Personal Choice	*Outside Pressure*
Eve	
Adam	

7. When Adam and Eve covered themselves, what feelings must have emerged for the first time?

8. From what you've read so far, speculate and answer these questions about God.

   a. Why did God want to keep Adam and Eve from the knowledge of good and evil?

   b. Why didn't God stop them from disobeying?

Hiding Out

When the first man and woman committed the first acts of disobedience, they felt the first negative emotions: guilt and shame. So they hid from God. Then when God found them, the husband and wife tried to pass the blame for their sin. Read how God responded:

> Then the man and his wife heard the sound of the LORD God as he was walking in the garden in the cool of the day, and they hid from the LORD God among the trees of the garden.
> But the LORD God called to the man, "Where are you?"
> He answered, "I heard you in the garden, and I was afraid because I was naked; so I hid."
> And he said, "Who told you that you were

naked? Have you eaten from the tree that I com-
manded you not to eat from?"

The man said, "The woman you put here
with me – she gave me some fruit from the tree,
and I ate it."

Then the LORD God said to the woman,
"What is this you have done?"

The woman said, "The serpent deceived
me, and I ate."

... The LORD God made garments of
skin for Adam and his wife and clothed them.
(Genesis 3:8-13,21)

9. Why do you think Adam and Eve were
   afraid of God?

10. After lovingly creating a perfect world for
    the people he loved, how do you suppose
    God felt about their disobedience?

11. Why do you think God clothed Adam
    and Eve?

Permanent Response

After this incident, God made the following
decision:

> *The LORD God said, "The man has now become like one of us, knowing good and evil. He must not also be allowed to reach out his hand and take also from the tree of life and eat, and live forever."* (Genesis 3:21-23)

12. Adam, Eve, and even the serpent suffered consequences for their actions. The Bible explains:

> *The LORD God said to the serpent, "Because you have done this, cursed are you above all the livestock and all the wild animals! . . . I will put enmity between you and the woman, and between your offspring and hers. . . ."*
> *To the woman he said, "I will greatly increase your pains in childbearing. . . . Your desire will be for your husband, and he will rule over you."*
> *To Adam he said, ". . . Cursed is the ground because of you; through painful toil you will eat of it all the days of your life."* (Genesis 3:14-17)

a. Why do you suppose God punished Adam, Eve, and the serpent?

b. Why do you think God chose these punishments?

c. How are these curses still evident today?

d. What pain do these punishments share in common?

Personal Effects

13. Compare Adam's and Eve's story to a time when you didn't act the way you wanted to or you deliberately did something wrong. How did you feel or act in the same way they did? Write a response for any of the following categories that apply.

- Disregard for what's already "good" in your life. (Adam and Eve had a perfect lifestyle.)

- Desire for the forbidden. (They wanted the one thing they couldn't have.)

- Desire for more power. (Increased knowledge meant more control.)

- Feelings of shame and fear. (They felt embarrassed before God and each other.)

- Running from the problem. (They hid from God.)

- Blaming others for personal actions. (Adam blamed Eve; she blamed the serpent.)

14. What have been the consequences of responding these ways?

Thinking Ahead

15. a. What would you like God to understand about the struggle with your wrong or disappointing actions?

   b. What would you like to understand about yourself?

Hopeful Words

Even though God punished Adam and Eve for their disobedience, he still loved them deeply. He still loves his creation, and believes it's "very good." And God still loves you, despite your shortcomings. The next lessons will reveal more about this love.

This week, read these Bible passages about God and his creation.

- Sunday: Genesis 1:1-26

- Monday: Psalm 23

- Tuesday: Psalm 121

- Wednesday: Psalm 136:1-9

- Thursday: Psalm 139:1-12

- Friday: Psalm 139:13-17

- Saturday: Psalm 149:1-5 ■

Whatever
Happened to Sin?

It could be lurking inside you.

M y Goal: *To accept personal responsibility for the sin I commit.*

Adam and Eve's story wasn't a creative tale to begin the Bible or an interesting way to explain humanity's inception. It's God's truth about how sin entered the world and affected the basic nature of people.

For centuries, philosophers have argued about whether humanity is basically "bad" or "good." In this lesson, you'll discover God's answer to their debate. But first, consider your opinion on this issue.

Personal Beliefs

1. a. What do you believe about the basic nature of humans? For example, are they basically good, bad, or both? Explain.

   b. In regard to your belief, how do you
      explain the bad things that people do?

2. How would you define sin?

Humanity's Downfall

Adam's and Eve's disobedience didn't end in
the garden. It affected the rest of their lives —
and the lives of every person since. Their actions
are often called "the downfall of humanity" or
just "the fall."

3. According to these Bible verses, how did
   Adam's and Eve's disobedience affect
   humanity? (The Bible often uses *man* or *men*
   for both men and women.)

*Sin entered the world through one man [Adam],
and death through sin, and in this way death
came to all men, because all sinned — for before
the law [Scripture] was given, sin was in the
world. . . .*

   *Nevertheless, death reigned from the time
of Adam . . . even over those who did not sin by
breaking a command, as Adam did.* (Romans
5:12-14)

4. After reading the following verses, summarize what the Bible says about humanity's dilemma with sin and God.

The LORD looks down from heaven on the sons of men to see if there are any who understand, any who seek God.
    All have turned aside, . . . there is no one who does good, not even one. (Psalm 14:2-3)

For all have sinned and fall short of the glory of God. (Romans 3:23)

5. Do you agree or disagree with the verses in question 4? Explain.

Meaning of Sin

If the Bible says humanity stands guilty of sin, we need to understand sin's nature. Webster's dictionary defines sin as "an offense against God."[1]

In the Old Testament of the Bible, the word translated as sin means "missing the mark" or standard that God set for humanity. In the New Testament, the word *sin* translates to "wrongdoing," "unrighteousness," or "injustice."[2]

6. After reading the following verses, summarize God's standard for humanity.

God said, "Be careful to obey all the law [commandments] my servant Moses gave you; do not turn from it to the right or to the left. . . . Do not let the Book of the Law depart from your mouth . . . so that you may be careful to do everything written in it." (Joshua 1:7-8)

Jesus replied: "'Love the Lord your God with all your heart and with all your soul and with all your mind.' This is the first and greatest commandment. And the second is like it: 'Love your neighbor as yourself.'" (Matthew 22:37-39)

7. How has humanity "missed the mark" that God set?

We all, like sheep, have gone astray, each of us has turned to his own way. (Isaiah 53:6)

8. How does the Bible's definition of sin compare with yours in question 2?

A Macro Look

The *law* or *commandments* mentioned in question 6 were given by God to Moses centuries ago. The basis of God's law rests on the Ten Commandments, stated below.

(1) *"You shall have no other gods before me."*

(2) *"You shall not make for yourself an idol in the form of anything."*

(3) *"You shall not misuse [swear with or treat flippantly] the name of the LORD your God."*

(4) *"Remember the Sabbath day [Sunday] by keeping it holy. . . . On it you shall not do any work."*

(5) *"Honor your father and your mother."*

(6) *"You shall not murder."*

(7) *"You shall not commit adultery."*

(8) *"You shall not steal."*

(9) *"You shall not give false testimony [lie] against your neighbor."*

(10) *"You shall not covet . . . anything that belongs to your neighbor."* (Exodus 20:3-4, 7-10,12-17)

9. Thinking about the world today, how do nations or societies break these commandments? Jot down an example for each command.

(1) Love no other gods.

(2) Do not make idols.

(3) Do not misuse God's name.

(4) Keep the Sabbath holy.

(5) Honor your parents.

(6) Do not murder.

(7) Do not commit adultery.

(8) Do not steal.

(9) Do not lie.

(10) Do not covet.

10. According to the following statement by the apostle Paul, a first-century Christian, why did God give commandments to humanity?

I would not have known what sin was except through the law. For I would not have known what coveting really was if the law had not said, "Do not covet." (Romans 7:7)

11. Below, read what the prophet Isaiah and Jesus Christ said about God's law. Then answer the questions that follow.

    Isaiah wrote, *"All men are like grass, and all their glory is like the flowers of the field. . . . The grass withers and the flowers fall, but the word of our God stands forever."* (Isaiah 40:6,8)

    Christ said, *"I tell you the truth, until heaven and earth disappear, not the smallest letter, not the least stroke of a pen, will by any means disappear from the Law."* (Matthew 5:18)

    a. How long will God's law endure?

    b. How long will God hold humanity responsible for his law?

A Micro Look

It's easy to see how the Ten Commandments apply to the world, but quite another matter to

44

take them personally. But God says all people break his commands, and consequently, everyone sins.

Christ taught that the commandments can be broken internally as well as externally. For example, he said:

> "You have heard that it was said, 'Do not commit adultery.' But I tell you that anyone who looks at a woman lustfully has already committed adultery with her in his heart." (Matthew 5:27)

12. Choose three commandments from page 41 and specify how they could be broken inwardly through words, thoughts, or attitudes.

Commandments	Internal Violations

13. Some people don't believe they're sinners because they say they've broken only one or two commandments. What insight does the following verse hold for them?

For whoever keeps the whole law and yet stumbles at just one point is guilty of breaking all of it. (James 2:10)

14. According to this next verse, what is our relationship to sin at birth? Why do you think this is so?

    Surely I was sinful at birth, sinful from the time my mother conceived me. (Psalm 51:5)

Unavoidable Conflict

God intended for people to be perfect, without sin. But Adam and Eve's disobedience led to the sinful downfall of humanity. We live with the desire to be good or perfect, but because of sin, we're unable to act the "right" way.

15. The apostle Paul, a leader of the early church, fought an internal battle between right and wrong. Read about his conflict in this excerpt from a letter he wrote to Christians:

    We know that the law is spiritual; but I am unspiritual, sold as a slave to sin. I do not understand what I do. For what I want to do I do not do, but what I hate to do. . . .

I know that nothing good lives in me,
that is, my sinful nature. For I have the desire
to do what is good, but I cannot carry it out.
(Romans 7:14-15,18)

a. Summarize Paul's conflict.

b. Do you identify with Paul's struggle?
   Why, or why not?

16. In your own words, how has this lesson
    enlightened your view of the following?

The struggle between good and evil:

The struggle to do what is right:

The existence of sin:

Personal responsibility for sin:

Good News

When Paul finished the lament about his sinful nature, he concluded:

> *What a wretched man I am! Who will rescue me from this body of death? Thanks be to God – through Jesus Christ our Lord!* (Romans 7:24-25)

Although Paul was a sinner, God forgave his sin. This forgiveness was granted through God's only Son, Jesus Christ. In the next lesson, you'll learn how to receive God's forgiveness for your sin, too.

This week, write out the Ten Commandments and ponder their significance. Then list a few ways you've broken these laws. After listing your personal infractions, ask yourself:

- How do I feel about the actions I've listed?

- Am I willing to take responsibility for my actions?

- How might taking this responsibility change my life? ■

NOTES
1. David B. Guralink, ed., *Webster's New World Dictionary* (New York: Simon and Schuster, 1982), page 1328.
2. Lawrence O. Richards, *Expository Dictionary of Bible Words* (Grand Rapids, MI: Zondervan, 1985), pages 566-567.

God Has a Better Idea

He can rescue you from yourself.

M *y Goal: To receive God's help for my struggle against sin and its consequences.*

A fallen humanity; personal responsibility for sin. These could paint a devastating picture—except for the forgiving brush strokes of God. He created a way to free people from sin and eternal punishment, and to change them in the deepest way possible.

Where we failed to help ourselves, God came to the rescue. In this lesson you'll learn about God, the rescuer. But first think about how you've tried rescuing yourself.

Personal Rescues

1. a. How have you tried to change personal actions you don't like?

b. To what extent have you succeeded in making these changes?

c. Would it be advantageous to enlist someone to help you make these changes? Why, or why not?

Sending Help

According to ancient Jewish law, God required his people to present a spotless lamb as a sacrifice to atone for their sins. When the lamb's blood was shed, God forgave the people's confessed sins. Without the sacrifice, God's holiness would not allow him to look on sin—let alone excuse it.

Following the same tradition, God sent his only Son, Jesus Christ, to earth to die for humanity's past, present, and future sin. Jesus was the only perfect one who could die for an evil world's sin and satisfy God's requirements for forgiveness.

2. As you read the Bible passage below, circle the words that describe humanity's condition before God.

You see, at just the right time, when we were still powerless, Christ died for the ungodly. . . . God demonstrates his own love for us in this: While we were still sinners, Christ died for us. (Romans 5:6,8)

a. Why do you think humanity is described as powerless?

b. What word would describe your struggle to change yourself? Explain.

3. According to this passage, what did Christ's death prove to humanity?

Paying Consequences

God dearly loved his Son, Jesus. He even spoke from heaven to say, "This is my Son, whom I love; with him I am well pleased" (Matthew 3:17).

God did not capriciously send Jesus to death. It was his only choice to save humanity—his beloved creation—from punishment and eternal suffering. God required a sinless sacrifice, and that meant painfully parting with his perfect Son.

John, a disciple of Jesus, explained it this way:

God so loved the world that he gave his one and only Son, that whoever believes in him shall not perish but have eternal life. (John 3:16)

4. Read the verse below, then answer the following questions.

For the wages of sin is death [eternity in hell], but the gift of God is eternal life [in heaven] in Christ Jesus our Lord. (Romans 6:23)

a. What are the consequences of sin?

b. What does God offer as a gift to us, in exchange for eternal death (suffering)?

c. Do you believe there is eternal death in hell and eternal life in heaven? Explain.

5. When Jesus died on the cross, what did he do for sinful humanity? In the following verses, circle all of the phrases or groups of words that apply.

*Surely he [Jesus] took up our infirmities and car-
ried our sorrows, yet we considered him stricken
by God, smitten by him, and afflicted.*

> *But he was pierced for our transgressions,
he was crushed for our iniquities; the punishment that brought us peace was upon him, and
by his wounds we are healed.*

> *. . . the LORD has laid on him the iniquity
of us all.* (Isaiah 53:4-6)

Narrow Escape

Christ shed his blood so we could escape the
punishment for our sin. The apostle Paul further
explained this to his readers:

> *Since we now have been justified by his [Jesus']
blood, how much more shall we be saved from
God's wrath through him! For if, when we
were God's enemies, we were reconciled to
him through the death of his Son, how much
more, having been reconciled, shall we be saved
through his life!*

> *Not only is this so, but we also rejoice in
God through our Lord Jesus Christ, through
whom we have now received reconciliation.*
(Romans 5:9-11)

6. a. Using a dictionary, define the words
below. Then reread the above passage,
amplifying it with your definitions.

Justified/justification:

Saved/salvation:

Reconciled/reconciliation:

b. Does this help you understand how Jesus Christ's death changed humanity's relationship with God? Explain.

7. The verses below further explain the results of Jesus' death.

God made him [Jesus] who had no sin to be sin for us, so that in him we might become the righteousness of God. (2 Corinthians 5:21)

For what the law was powerless to do in that it was weakened by the sinful nature, God did by sending his own Son in the likeness of sinful man to be a sin offering.

And so he condemned sin in sinful man, in order that the righteous requirements of the law might be fully met in us. (Romans 8:3-4)

a. Why was Jesus able to reconcile sinful people to God?

b. Using the dictionary again, define *righteous/righteousness*.

c. Why did God want sinful humanity to become righteous through Jesus?

Accepting the Gift

Three days after his death, Jesus rose from the grave and lived on the earth a while longer. Then he ascended to heaven to dwell with God the Father again. When Jesus resurrected from the dead, he conquered humanity's sin and its awful consequences. He took the punishment for us, so someday, we can live with him forever.

Because of Jesus' death and resurrection, we can receive God's forgiveness. It's as simple as reaching out and receiving a free gift. However, receivers must allow this gift to change them.

8. a. Using the dictionary, define the word *grace* in light of the following Bible passage.

For it is by grace you have been saved,
through faith – and this not from yourselves,
it is the gift of God – not by works, so that no
one can boast. (Ephesians 2:8-9)

b. Do the above verses alter your view of
how people are saved from sin? Why, or
why not?

9. Paul also taught how to accept God's free
gift of salvation from sin:

If you confess with your mouth, "Jesus is Lord,"
and believe in your heart that God raised him
from the dead, you will be saved.
*   For it is with your heart that you believe*
and are justified, and it is with your mouth that
you confess and are saved. (Romans 10:9-10)

a. What part do each of these play in being
saved from sin?

Heart:

Mouth:

b. Look up the word *Lord* in the dictionary
and write a definition below.

c. What would it mean for someone to
make Jesus the Lord of her life?

10. What else must be confessed to receive
salvation?

*Repent [of your sins], then, and turn to God, so
that your sins may be wiped out.* (Acts 3:19)

Escaping Punishment

To genuinely repent of sin is to have a "change
of mind" about your life's direction. It is
deciding to make the changes necessary to dis-
card a sinful lifestyle.

In the Old Testament, *repent* means "to
regret" or "to turn from a previous way." The
New Testament definition reinforces this meaning by emphasizing "a change of mind and
attitude."[1]

The Bible tells us how repentance should be approached:

Godly sorrow brings repentance that leads to salvation and leaves no regret, but worldly sorrow brings death. (2 Corinthians 7:10)

11. What would be the difference between godly sorrow and worldly sorrow? What are the results of each?

Definition	Results
Godly Sorrow	
Worldly Sorrow	

12. What will happen if we ignore God's free gift of salvation and refuse to repent?

If . . . every violation and disobedience received its just punishment, how shall we escape if we ignore such a great salvation? (Hebrews 2:2-3)

The present heavens and earth are reserved for fire, being kept for the day of judgment and destruction of ungodly men [people].

[But] the Lord [God] . . . is patient with you, not wanting anyone to perish, but everyone to come to repentance. (2 Peter 3:7,9)

13. a. Does God want his creation (people) to receive punishment? Explain.

   b. It is often said, "God loves sinners but hates their sin." How is this concept supported by the verses in question 12?

14. When is a good time to accept salvation?

God said, "In the time of favor I heard you, and in the day of salvation I helped you."

I tell you, now is the time of God's favor, now is the day of salvation. (2 Corinthians 6:2)

Deciding Soon

God will help us in our day of salvation and all the days of our lives. But first, we must accept his gift to us.

This week, consider these steps to receive salvation, and how they would change your life. Then if you choose to receive Jesus as your Savior, write a prayer that incorporates these steps.

- **Confess** your sin and rebelliousness toward God.

- **Repent** of your sin, choosing to change in a way that forsakes it.

- **Ask** God to forgive you of your sin.

- **Accept** God's forgiveness and free gift of salvation.

- **Acknowledge** Jesus as the Lord of your life.

Your Prayer

_____   _____

Signed   Date ■

NOTE
1. Lawrence O. Richards, *Expository Dictionary of Bible Words* (Grand Rapids, MI: Zondervan Publishing, 1985), page 522.

You Can Change for the Better

There's help for personal struggles.

M y Goal: To allow God's power to help me change for the better.

Accepting God's salvation doesn't make us perfect, even though we'd love to be flawless. As
long as we live in a broken world, we'll grapple
with imperfection.

But when we accept God's salvation, he
infuses us with power through his Spirit so
we can change for the better. This lesson will
explain how God can help you change from the
inside out. Begin by expressing what you think
about changing.

Hoping for Change

1. a. What would be the most difficult thing to
   change about yourself?

b. Do you believe God can help you change? Explain.

A Clean Slate

The following verses explain what happens when someone accepts Jesus Christ as Savior.

> *In your love you [God] kept me from the pit of destruction; you have put all my sins behind your back.* (Isaiah 38:17)

> *Therefore, if anyone is in Christ, he is a new creation; the old has gone, the new has come!* (2 Corinthians 5:17)

2. a. What would you say characterizes a "new creation"?

b. What "old" would be put away and what "new" would come to a believer in Jesus?

3. When we repent and accept God's gift of salvation, he wipes our slate clean of past sins. How would it feel to start life "fresh," with God putting our sins "behind his back"?

New Life

In addition to forgiveness of sins, Jesus says that he gives life to his followers.

> Jesus said, *"I am come that they may have life, and have it to the full."* (John 10:10)

4. What would be a "full life" for you? Consider these aspects: emotional, spiritual, physical, mental, relational.

Power for Living

After forgiving their sins, God places his Holy Spirit inside believers to give them the power to live in a way that's pleasing to him. We're not left alone to face ourselves; the Spirit guides and comforts us along the way.

5. Why does the Holy Spirit reside in those who have placed their faith in Jesus? Read these verses, then complete the sentences that follow.

Through Christ Jesus the law of the Spirit of life set me free from the law of sin and death. (Romans 8:2)

We . . . are being transformed into his [Jesus'] likeness with ever-increasing glory, which comes from the Lord, who is the Spirit. (2 Corinthians 3:18)

"The Counselor, the Holy Spirit, whom the Father will send in my [Jesus'] name, will teach you all things and will remind you of everything I have said to you." (John 14:26)

God's Holy Spirit can keep us free from . . .

God's Spirit helps us become more like . . .

God's Spirit teaches us to . . .

6. Read the following passage, then compare the differences between those who "live by God's Spirit" and those who do not.

Those who live according to the sinful nature
have their minds set on what that nature desires;
but those who live in accordance with the Spirit
have their minds set on what the Spirit desires.
    . . . the mind controlled by the Spirit is
life and peace; the sinful mind is hostile toward
God. It does not submit to God's law, nor can it
do so. . . .
    You, however, are controlled not by the sin-
ful nature but by the Spirit, if the Spirit of God
lives in you. (Romans 8:5-7,9)

Sinful Nature	*God's Spirit*
Where the mind is set:	
Evident feelings:	
Response to God's law:	

Personal Changes

Jesus said that faith is necessary for a person to be able to make "impossible" changes.

> *"I tell you the truth, if you have faith as small as a mustard seed . . . nothing will be impossible for you."* (Matthew 17:20)

7. Using your dictionary, define the word *faith*.

8. a. To change, what must we be willing to do? Circle your answer.

   > *Thanks be to God that, though you used to be slaves to sin, you wholeheartedly obeyed the form of teaching [in the Bible] to which you were entrusted.* (Romans 6:17)

   b. What will God do? Circle his promise and its result in the verse below.

   > *God has said, "Never will I leave you; never will I forsake you." So we say with confidence, "The Lord is my helper; I will not be afraid."* (Hebrews 13:5-6)

9. On the next page, read how the Holy Spirit can change people from the inside out. Then complete the sentences, supplying the Bible's words on the left side and your words on the right side. The first one is completed as an example.

The fruit [or results] of the Spirit [in the believer's life] is love, joy, peace, patience, kindness, goodness, faithfulness, gentleness and self-control. (Galatians 5:22)

a. The Holy Spirit gives people . . .

_____*Love*_____ to replace ____*hatred*____.

_____ instead of _____.

_____ to overcome _____.

_____ and not _____.

_____ rather than _____.

_____ as opposed to _____.

_____ in the midst of _____.

_____ in exchange for _____.

_____ to replace _____.

b. How could these characteristics of God's Spirit help a person change for the better?

10. a. What qualities does the Spirit give to those who are hesitant or afraid about the changes they need to make? Circle them in the verse below.

God did not give us a spirit of timidity [fear], but a spirit of power, of love and of self-discipline. (2 Timothy 1:7)

b. How would each of those qualities be helpful in making personal changes?

Daily Remembrances

The Christian life is a day-by-day, step-by-step walk with God. Instead of relying on our unpredictable selves, we depend on a trustworthy God.

11. There are daily disciplines that can help Christians change for the better. Read the verses below, then summarize their content with the sentence completions that follow.

How can a young man [person] keep his way pure? By living according to your [God's] word. I seek you with all my heart. . . . I have hidden your word in my heart that I might not sin against you. (Psalm 119:9-11)

"If you believe, you will receive whatever you ask for in prayer." (Matthew 21:22)

So faith comes from hearing, and hearing by the word of Christ. (Romans 10:17, NASB)

If we confess our sins, He [God] is faithful and righteous to forgive us our sins and to cleanse us from all unrighteousness. (1 John 1:9, NASB)

We can read and follow God's word (the Bible) to . . .

We can pray to . . .

We can gain faith by . . .

We can receive forgiveness for sin by . . .

12. Even though God's Spirit resides in us, what must we remember about mortality?

   Therefore we do not lose heart, but though our outer man [person] is decaying, yet our inner man [person] is being renewed day by day. (2 Corinthians 4:16, NASB)

13. The next verse tells us what we can look forward to in heaven. What special meaning does this have for you?

*"He [God] will wipe every tear from their eyes.
There will be no more death or mourning or cry-
ing or pain. . . . I am making everything new!"*
(Revelation 21:4-5)

14. a. Turn back to lesson 1 and read question
       13 (pages 34-35). How might God help
       you with the actions that you listed?

    b. Choose one action that bothers you the
       most. With God's help, how can you
       begin changing it?

Continuing On
This week, read "Starting a New Life" on the
next pages. It will help you further understand
the Holy Spirit's relationship to Christians. ■

Starting a New Life
How God's Spirit helps you change.

W hen you ask Christ to become your Savior, he doesn't expect you to muddle through life on your own. His Holy Spirit will help you change for the better.

Author Michael Griffiths described this process in his book *God Is Great, God Is Good, I'd Believe Him If I Could*. To learn how the Holy Spirit can enrich your life, read the following excerpt from Griffiths' book.

□ □ □

More Than Born Again
There is much more to this new spiritual life than being born again as real Christians or discovering how real Jesus is. As we open our hearts to Christ and let him indwell us by his Spirit, we find out that he also works inside us to make us holy and to make us like himself.

"Through Christ Jesus the law of the Spirit of life set me free from the law of sin and death" (Romans 8:2). You can understand this verse by imagining that you are a person who has been

infected with a fatal disease. The body's defense system has been swamped and you, the patient, are dying. You hurry to the doctor and ask him to save you. He fills the syringe with an antibiotic and injects this substance into you, which fights against the disease and destroys it.

Romans 8:2 reminds us that sin, the inward moral disease of the heart, is destroying us. We cry to Christ for help: "Please save me!" and he puts into us the new principle of life through the Spirit to overcome the power of sin within us. Just as a battle goes on between the antibiotic and the disease-causing bacteria, so a struggle goes on between the Holy Spirit and sin as he systematically overcomes the moral disease in our hearts.

Progressive Recovery

It is not that we experience instant perfection the moment we become Christians any more than a patient is immediately restored to blooming health the very moment when the doctor injects him. It is a much more progressive convalescence, as the disease is eradicated and the damage that it has done is gradually repaired. You are saved the moment you are in the doctor's hands, but you are not yet totally recovered. The seventeenth-century writer Richard Baxter once said that "the church is a mere hospital."

Christians are not, therefore, people who feel themselves to be better than other people. Quite the reverse. They are people who, recognizing their sickness and their need of treatment, have run to Christ and asked him to save them. Christians are "in-patients" in Christ's hospital, calling encouragingly through the windows, saying, "Come and try this doctor! We've found that he has the cure for our moral diseases. We're not totally recovered yet, but we're glad that we've put ourselves in his hands to treat us, and we urge you to do the same."

Let's continue with the injection analogy just a bit further. Vaccines are often prepared by taking serum from an animal that has deliberately been infected by disease and has overcome it. These victorious antibodies are then given to the victim in order that the same victory might be repeated. The Spirit, who is received when someone becomes a Christian, is the Spirit of Christ, who lived a perfect human life, victorious over all temptation, and who has decisively defeated sin on the cross. We are asking Christ, who has overcome sin himself, to overcome sin in us right now through his Spirit.

Technical Terms

What I have been describing in these recent paragraphs is what is technically called sanctification: the process by which Christians, by trusting in Jesus, become increasingly conformed to that pattern of perfect human life that he has set before us.

Notice here, incidentally, the contrast between the Christian religion and many other religions that see salvation as an ultimate goal to be attained by a sufficiently meritorious life. Such religions provide a set of external rules that, if observed, claim to guarantee salvation.

By contrast, the Christian life offers salvation to start with. The moment we have put ourselves into the Doctor's hands we are safe! The transformed life is the consequence of having been saved by Jesus, not the ground on which salvation may be ultimately achieved. It is not that we become Christians by adherence to an external set of ethical rules, but *rather that we are progressively transformed by the indwelling Spirit to become like Jesus.*

Thus, being a Christian is not a question of "Live a good life and then you'll be saved," but rather the reverse, which says, "First be saved and then the Savior will enable you to lead a new life through his indwelling Spirit."

Final Destination

It may be that many of us hesitate to become Christians for fear that we might fail. We don't want to be wishy-washy, feeble, uncommitted Christians. Nor do we want to give up halfway. How can we be certain that after having put our trust in Christ we will continue to live faithfully as Christians? Won't there be all kinds of irresistible temptations?

I remember the very first time my wife and I returned by ship from Japan to Britain. We had been on board for five weeks and now, one cold, blustery January morning, through the sleet and murk, we could dimly make out the windswept coast of Torbay. There had been times when we wondered whether we would ever see our native land again. And even now, was it possible that in the next few hours we might meet some fatal disaster and perish?

And then . . . pocketa-pocketa, pocketa-pocketa, pocketa-pocketa . . . a little boat came chugging out from Brixham and struggled alongside the liner, swinging up and down in the waves. The pilot leaped from the deck of the tug to a rope ladder and came on board, expressly in order to see that we would arrive safely at Tilbury Docks, avoiding wrecks, rocks, the Goodwin Sands, and many other hazards we did not even notice.

In the same way, God has given us his Holy

Spirit to indwell us, to see that our salvation is safely completed, and to guide us safely to our destination. . . . The Holy Spirit has been sent down to be right alongside us on earth, in order to ensure that we will arrive safely at our heavenly destination.[1]

—MICHAEL GRIFFITHS

□ □ □

Spirit in You

1. In one sentence, summarize the Holy Spirit's work in a Christian's life.

2. How would you like the Holy Spirit to transform you?

3. What must you do to experience this transformation?

4. What would you still like to understand about the Holy Spirit?

5. How could you learn more about the Holy
   Spirit? ■

NOTE

1. Article excerpted and adapted from *God Is Great, God Is
   Good, I'd Believe Him If I Could* by Michael Griffiths (Colorado
   Springs, CO: NavPress, 1987), pages 119-123. British edition:
   Down to Earth God (East Sussex, England: Hodder and
   Stoughton). Used with permission of Edward England Books
   Literary Agency.

Learning to Believe

Books about the personal God.

Bonhoffer, Dietrich. *The Cost of Discipleship*. New York: Macmillan, 1963.

Couchman, Judith. *Getting a Grip on Guilt*. Colorado Springs, CO: NavPress, 1990.

Graham, Billy. *How to Be Born Again*. Irving, TX: Word, 1977.

Lewis, C. S. *Mere Christianity*. New York: Macmillan, 1952.

Little, Paul. *Know Why You Believe*. Downers Grove, IL: InterVarsity Press, 1968.

Menninger, Karl. *Whatever Became of Sin?* New York: Bantam Books, 1984.

Schaeffer, Francis. *He Is There and He Is Not Silent.* Wheaton, IL: Tyndale House, 1972.

Schaeffer, Francis. *The God Who Is There.* Downers Grove, IL: InterVarsity Press, 1968.

Tournier, Paul. *The Meaning of Persons.* San Francisco, CA: Harper and Row, Publishers, 1957.

White, John. *The Cost of Commitment.* Downers Grove, IL: InterVarsity Press, 1976.

White, John. *The Fight.* Downers Grove, IL: InterVarsity Press, 1976. ∎

AUTHOR

J udith Couchman has published many times in magazines and curriculum publications. In addition to this study book, she's also published *Getting a Grip on Guilt* and *Why Is Her Life Better Than Mine?* (NavPress).

Judith is Director of Communications for The Navigators and also develops new products for NavPress. She is the former editor of *Sunday Digest* and *Christian Life*, and has worked as a public relations professional and a journalism teacher. She has also taught writing at conferences around the United States.

Judith has received top awards from the Evangelical Press Association, the International Association of Business Communicators, the Advertising Federation, and several high school press associations. She's also listed in *Who's Who of Female Executives*.

She holds a B.S. in education and an M.A. in journalism, collects art by "people who aren't famous yet," and lives in Colorado Springs, Colorado. ■

ABOUT THIS SERIES

O ther study booklets in the *QUESTIONS WOMEN ASK* series are:

Can I Really Have It All? by Maxine Hancock. Discover the real meaning of success and fulfillment.

If My Kids Drive Me Crazy, Am I a Bad Mom? by Janet Chester Bly. How to make the most of the mothering years.

Is Your To-Do List About to Do You In? by Marlene LeFever. Sort out and reduce the stresses of everyday living.

Why Do I Always Play It So Safe? by Evelyn Bence. Move past your fears toward the freedom to pursue your dreams.

Will the Pain Ever Go Away? by Alice Lawson Cox. Help for the woman who is working through pain and grief.

These studies can be purchased at a Christian bookstore. Or order a catalog from NavPress, Customer Services, P. O. Box 6000, Colorado Springs, CO 80934. Or call 1-800-366-7788 for information. ■